Loving God

Bernard of Clairvaux

REJUVENATED BOOKS

Series One

Loving God
Rejuvenated Books: Series One
ISBN: 978-1-63171-001-8

About this text: Sometime between 1125 and 1141, Bernard of Clairvaux wrote this book at the request of a close friend. It has been in print ever since, both in the original French and in a variety of English translations. This paraphrase is based two of those English translations:

> Bernard of Clairvaux. *Saint Bernard on the Love of God.* Translated by Marianne C. Patmore and Coventry Patmore. 2nd ed. London: Burns and Oates, 1884.

> Bernard of Clairvaux. *Saint Bernard on Loving God.* Translated by William B. van Allen. Tenby, South Wales: Caldey Abbey, 1909.

This book is printed in the United States of America.

Contents

I HAVE SAID ENOUGH to show how much we should love God and that he deserves our love. But who really understands how much God deserves our love? Who has words for that?

Dedication

To the illustrious Lord Haimeric, Cardinal Deacon of the Roman Church and Chancellor. From Bernard, called Abbot of Clairvaux, wishing you long life in the Lord and death in the Lord.

In the past, you have sought prayers from me, not the solving of problems. I consider myself sufficient for neither. If my conversation does not reveal that, then my profession does, and to tell the truth, I lack the diligence and the ability that are most essential to that task. However, I am glad that you turn to me again for spiritual counsel instead of busying yourself about worldly matters. I only wish you had gone to someone better equipped than me.

Even so, the learned and the simple give the same excuse, and one can hardly tell whether the excuse comes from modesty or ignorance unless obedience to the assigned task reveals which it is. Therefore, take from my poverty whatever I can give you, lest I should seem to play the philosopher through my silence.

I do not promise to answer the other questions that you have raised. As for this question about loving God, however, I will answer as God teaches me. This question is the sweetest, it can be handled most safely, and it will be most beneficial. You must save your other questions for wiser men.

ONE

Why and How
We Should Love God

You ask me to explain why and how we should love God. I answer that God himself is the reason we should love him. The scope of our love for him should have no limit. Is this clear enough?

It might be clear enough for a learned person. However, I want to answer for both the learned and unlearned, so although I may have said enough for the former, I must remember others. For them, I will unfold my meaning in greater detail — though perhaps not in greater depth.

Two things motivate us to love God for his own sake. First, nothing is more reasonable, and second, nothing is more beneficial. When one asks why we should love God, the question may have either of two meanings: How does God deserve our love? How do we benefit from loving God? The answer to both questions is the same. The reason to love God is God.

Let's first consider why God deserves our love. No claim to our love can be stronger than this, that in spite of our great unworthiness, God gave himself to us. Being God, what could he give us that is more valuable than himself? If then by the question of why we should love God, we mean to ask what *right* he has to our love, the clearest answer is simply that "he first loved us." This gives him a right to our love in return.

Consider the one who loves us. Consider whom he loves. Consider how much he loves us.

The one who loves us is the one about whom every spirit testifies: "You are my Lord. Apart from you, I have no good thing." His love is sincere because he loves with a love that never seeks its own interests.

To whom has such wonderful love been given? The apostle answers: "While we were yet God's enemies, we were reconciled to him through the death of his Son." God has freely given his love to us while we were still his enemies.

How great is his love? John answers: "God loved the world so much that he gave his one and only son." Paul adds: "He did not spare his own son but gave him up for us all." Of himself, the son says, "No one has greater love than this, that someone lays down his life for his friends."

The infinitely holy, sovereign, and almighty God therefore deserves to be loved by the infinitely wicked, small, and weak human. One might say, "Yes, this is true for humans but not for angels." For angels, however, this great sacrifice was not necessary. He who has helped us in our misery has kept the angels from falling into the same. God's love has provided us with a way of escape, and the same love has protected the angels from a fall like ours.

Two

God's Right to Our Love

Those who acknowledge the truth of what I have said must surely acknowledge that God should be loved because he deserves our love.

If unbelievers will not accept these facts, God immediately refutes their ingratitude with the unlimited gifts that he lavishes upon us, body and soul. For who else gives us the food that we eat, the light that we see, the air that we breathe? It would be foolish to even try to list all of his gifts, for they are countless. It is enough to name the main ones — food, sun, and air. I mention these not because I consider them the greatest of his gifts but because they are the most necessary. The body cannot survive without them.

For the greatest of his gifts, we must look to the soul, the superior part of our being. Those gifts are dignity, intelligence, and virtue. When I speak of dignity in people, I mean the free will that is in us. This is what raises us above all other living creatures and places them under our dominion. Intelligence reveals this dignity to us, and at the same time, it reveals that it is no accomplishment of our own. Virtue drives us to hungrily seek the one whose creation we are and, when we have found him, to embrace him passionately.

These three gifts each have a double nature. Dignity can be viewed as the exclusive property of human beings, but it is also the power of dominion, the reason for the fear that humans have always produced in every other living creature. Intelligence is also two-fold. It perceives that this dignity and other natural qualities are within us, but it also sees that we do not create them for ourselves. Lastly, virtue also has a double nature. It spurs us to seek the one to whom we owe our existence. When we have found him, it moves us to cling to him so tightly that we cannot be separated. Because of their two-fold nature, dignity without intelligence is worthless, and intelligence without virtue can only do harm, as I will explain.

There is no reward in having a gift unless you know that you have it. However, if you know what you have but then ignore the fact that this gift does not exist through its own power but through the power of another, you take pride in yourself and not in God. Paul asks, "What do you have that was not given to you? And if it was given to you, why do you boast as if it were not given?" He does not merely say, "Why do you boast?" He adds, "as if it were not given?"

This shows that is it not wrong to boast about having something. It is wrong to ignore the fact that this something is a gift you received. Such pride is rightly called "vanity" because it is not founded on the solid rock of truth. The apostle distinguishes this vain pride from acceptable pride by saying, "The one who boasts can boast in the

Lord." That kind of boasting is taking pride in the truth because God is truth. You must see, then, that there are two things to understand. First, we are what we are, and second, we have not created ourselves.

If we overlook either idea, then we will either take no pride in ourselves or the pride we take in ourselves will be vanity. As it's written, "If you do not understand, most beautiful of women, follow the tracks of the sheep." In truth, this is what happens. When people do not understand their own dignity, then because of this ignorance, they can rightly be compared to the beasts with whom they share the decaying and mortal nature of this world. Not understanding themselves, people—who are distinguished from irrational animals by their ability to understand—begin to mingle with the animals until gradually they lose sight of the glory that is within themselves and occupy themselves with outward, sensual things. Led on by curiosity, they lower themselves to the level of beasts

Loving God

because they do not understand that they have
received more than the other animals.

We must constantly guard against this kind
of ignorance. We must by no means think
of ourselves as less than what God has made
us. With even greater care, we must avoid
that greater ignorance of attributing more to
ourselves than we possess, which is what we do
when we mistakenly attribute to ourselves the
gifts that we perceive. Beyond these two kinds
of ignorance, we must even more detest and
flee from the presumption that would lead us
to knowingly and purposefully take pride in the
gifts that we perceive. We know full well that the
good in us does not come from ourselves. When
we take pride in it, we shamelessly rob God of
the honor that we owe him.

In the first case, we have no pride at all. In
the second case, we have pride but not in God.
In the third case, we no longer sin ignorantly but
deliberately by usurping the honor that belongs
to God alone. This latter arrogance is far greater

than the second fault because while the second fault does not recognize God, this arrogance despises him. Ignorance turns us into beasts, but this arrogance turns us into devils. Only pride, the greatest of all sins, can cause us to use the gifts we have received as if they were naturally ours and then rob our benefactor, for our own sake, of the honor we owe him.

Therefore, in addition to dignity and intelligence, we must add virtue, which is the fruit of both. Through virtue, we search for and find the generous author of all things, the one who must in all good things be glorified. Without virtue, then like the servant "who knows the master's will and does not get ready or does not do what the master wants," people will be "beaten with many blows." Why? Because "they commit themselves to a sinful course and do not reject what is wrong" and, worse, "even on their beds, they plot evil." Like the wicked servant, they appropriate the honor that their good master should have received even though they understand, through the gift of intelligence, that they themselves have no claim to it.

It is clear, then, that dignity without intelligence is useless, and intelligence without virtue is damnable. However, to those who possess virtue, neither dignity nor intelligence can be harmful. They lift up their voices and praise God, joyfully singing, "Not to us, Lord, not to us, but to your name be the glory." In other words, "We take no credit for our dignity or our intelligence. We give all the honor to you, for from you we have received all that we have."

I have wandered a bit in order to show you that even those who do not know Christ are sufficiently instructed — both by natural law and by they gifts they possess, body and soul — to love God for God's own sake. Now I will summarize in a few words.

Where are the unbelievers who do not understand that from God alone, who "makes his sun rise on the evil and on the good and sends rain on the just and on the unjust," they have received all that is necessary for life—light, air, and food? And who, no matter how worldly, can attribute the dignity of the human race to anyone but the one who says in Genesis, "Let us make mankind in our image, in our likeness"? Who sees the author of intelligence as anyone but the one "who teaches man knowledge"? Who can give us virtue other than the Lord of virtue?

God then deserves to be loved for his own sake, even based on the knowledge of those who know themselves but do not know Christ. All people, including unbelievers, have no excuse but to love the Lord their God with all their heart, all their soul, and all their strength. An innate justice, which can be seen by intelligence, cries out from the depths of their souls that they are bound to love the one from whom they receive all things. However, it is very difficult—impossible for humans—to give all the honor to God through natural strength or the power of free will. Instead, we keep some praise for ourselves, as it is written, "For all people look out for their own interests," and elsewhere, "Every inclination of the human heart is evil from childhood."

THREE

Why Believers Should Love God

Believers understand well enough how completely they need Jesus and his sacrifice. While they wonder at and embrace "the love that surpasses knowledge," they feel ashamed at failing to give even what little they can offer — nothing but their souls — in return for this great love and honor. "Whoever has been forgiven little loves little," but the believers love more because they understand how much they are loved.

Neither Jews nor unbelievers feel the pangs of love that the church feels. She sings, "Strengthen me with raisin cakes, refresh me with apples, for

I am faint with love." She sees Solomon wearing the crown that his mother placed on his head. She sees the only son of the Father staggering under the weight of the cross, the God of all majesty discolored with bruises and covered with spit. She sees the author of life and glory hung by nails, pierced with a spear, overwhelmed with mockery, and then giving his precious soul for his friends. Gazing upon this, she feels the sword of love pierce her heart, making her cry out again, "Strengthen me with raisin cakes, refresh me with apples, for I am faint with love!"

The fruits that the bride gathers in the garden of her beloved are pomegranates from the Tree of Life. These taste like the bread of heaven, and their color is like the blood of Christ. She sees death receive its deathblow and death's author overthrown. She sees the victor rising gloriously, leading the captives from hell to earth and from earth to heaven, so that "at the name of Jesus, every knee shall bow, in heaven and on earth and under the earth."

Under the ancient curse, the earth was doomed to bear nothing but thorns and weeds, but now the church sees the earth covered with flowers, restored by the grace of a new blessing. As she remembers these words, "My heart leaps for joy, and with my song I praise him," she is strengthened by the fruit that she gathers from the tree of the cross and by the flowers of the resurrection, whose divine perfume invites the frequent visits of her beloved.

She cries out, "Oh, how handsome you are, my lover! How delightful you are! Our bed is lush and green!" By speaking of her bed, she reveals what she desires, and by speaking of its lushness, she shows that her hope is not based on her own merits but on the flowers picked from the field that God has blessed.

Christ, who chose to be born and brought up at Nazareth, the city of branches, delights in such blossoms. Drawn by their fragrance, the heavenly bridegroom willingly and often enters the inner chamber of the heart that is adorned with these fruits and flowers. When he sees a mind thoughtfully considering the fruit of his suffering and the glorious flowers of his resurrection, he is willingly and joyfully present.

We see that the symbols of his suffering and sacrifice are like last year's fruit, which was ripening during the ages of sin and death until "the fullness of time had come." However, the symbols of his resurrection are like this year's flowers, which bloom in the new summertime of grace that he has brought to the earth. At the general resurrection, when time will be no more, the abundance of their fruit will infinite. As it is written, "See! The winter is past. The rains are over and gone. Flowers appear on the earth." This shows us that summer has come back with the one who transformed the icy winter of death into the spring of new life. He says, "See! I make all things new!" His body, which was sown in death, has blossomed in the resurrection. In the same way, our own barren fields become green with new grass. Our coldness begins to warm. What was dead in us comes back to life.

The father of the one who makes all things new takes great pleasure in the freshness of these flowers, the ripeness of these fruits, and the beauty of this garden that breathes out such exquisite perfume. It blesses him, and like Isaac, he might say, "Ah, the smell of my son is like the smell of a field that the Lord has blessed." This field is full to overflowing, for it is "from his fullness that we have all received, grace upon grace." But the bride may come whenever she pleases to gather these flowers and fruits. With them, she adorns the innermost chambers of her conscience so that the bridegroom, when he arrives, will find the little bed of her heart enlivened with the sweetest perfume.

If we want Christ to be a frequent visitor, we must thus fill our hearts with thoughts of his death and resurrection and with faithful contemplation of the mercy he showed in dying for us and of the mighty power he demonstrated in rising from the dead. As David says, "One thing God has spoken, two things I have heard: 'Power belongs to God, and to you, O Lord, belongs unfailing love.'" The testimony of these two things is always convincing. Christ died to remove our sins and rose from the dead to make us righteous before God. He ascended to heaven to protect us, sent his Holy Spirit to comfort and encourage us, and will come again for our complete fulfillment. In his death, we have proof of his mercy. In his resurrection, we have proof of his power. In the rest, we see both his mercy and his power united.

The bride asks to be strengthened with raisin cakes and refreshed with apples because she knows how easily the warmth of love can cool and fade. However, she only seeks such refreshment until she is brought into the chambers of her beloved. Then he will cover her with the caresses she has longed for, and she will cry out, "His left hand is under my head, and his right hand embraces me!" She will feel how the embrace of his right hand surpasses all other sweetness — surpasses even the first touch of his left hand, with which he caressed her in the first days of his arrival.

She will understand then that "it is the Spirit who gives life, that the flesh is no help at all." She will see the meaning of his words: "For my spirit is sweeter than honey. My inheritance is sweeter than honey and the honeycomb." When the psalmist writes, "They will pour forth the fame of your abundant goodness," he undoubtedly refers to what he has just written: "One generation will commend your works to another. They will tell of your mighty acts."

On earth, we have the memory of the bridegroom. In heaven, we will have his eternal presence. His presence is the joy of those who have already arrived in port. His memory is the comfort of us who are still travelers, buffeted by the waves and journeying toward our homeland.

FOUR

The Contemplation of God

It is important to consider who finds comfort in the contemplation of God. It is certainly not the crooked and stubborn people to whom Jesus said, "But woe to you who are rich, for you have already received your comfort." It is instead those who can truthfully say, "When I was in distress, I sought the Lord. At night, I stretched out untiring hands, and I would not be comforted." It is fitting that those who aren't satisfied by the present should fix their gaze upon the future, that those who refuse to be comforted by the stream of earthly pleasure should be comforted by the hope of eternal joy. These are the people who seek the Lord, who do not search for their own advancement but for the face of the God of Jacob.

The contemplation of God is sweetest to those who sigh for him, who with every breath think about his presence. However, far from satisfying their hunger for him, contemplation increases it, just as scripture testifies: "Those who eat me will yet be hungry, and those who drink me will yet be thirsty." The hungry one might say, "When I awake, I will be satisfied with seeing your likeness." Yes, and "blessed are those who hunger and thirst for righteousness, for they alone will be satisfied."

But woe to you, wicked and degraded people. Woe to you, foolish and stupid people who hate the memory of Christ yet fear his presence. You have good reason to fear, for even now you have not desired to escape the snares of the one who hunts you. As it is written, "Those who desire to be rich fall into temptation, into a snare, into many senseless and harmful desires that plunge them into ruin and destruction." On that day, you will not escape this terrifying and hopeless judgment: "Depart from me, you cursed ones, into the eternal fire prepared for the devil and his angels."

What a fearful judgment that is, so much harder to bear than the sweet, tender promise that the church gives every day when it remembers Christ's sacrifice: "Whoever eats my flesh and drinks my blood has eternal life." In other words, everyone who honors his death by following his example and "putting to death everything that is earthly" within themselves will have eternal life. As Paul says, "If we endure hardship for him, we will also reign with him." Nevertheless, even to this day, many who hear those words turn away and leave in sorrow, saying by their actions rather than their mouths, "This is a hard saying. Who can bear it?"

They put their trust in earthly riches. They are a generation "whose heart is not steadfast, whose spirit is not faithful to God." They can't stand even the mention of the cross. The thought of Christ's suffering is intolerable. How will they ever be able to endure that terrible judgment to depart from Christ and go to the eternal fire that awaits the devil and his angels? When this stone falls on them, it will "crush them to powder."

However, "the generation of the upright will be blessed." Like the apostle, their only goal is "to please him, whether at home in the body or away from it." They will hear this judgment: "Come, you who are blessed by my Father. Receive your inheritance, the kingdom that was prepared for you since the creation of the world."

On that day, those who have not kept their hearts pure will understand, too late, how easy Christ's yoke is compared to the sorrow they must endure and how light the burden is that they refused to bear, as if it were a rough and heavy load. You poor, miserable slaves of the world! You must understand that you cannot put your confidence in the cross of our Lord Jesus Christ and at the same time devote yourself to worldly riches. You cannot taste the sweetness of our Lord while you hunger for gold. If the thought of him has never been your joy, then the day of his coming will be a day of judgment for you.

The believing soul longs with all her heart for God. She rests peacefully in the contemplation of her beloved. She takes pride in the disgrace of the cross until she can see her savior face to face. She is like the dove of Christ, whose wings "are sheathed with silver," white with innocence and purity, resting in the thought of his abundant goodness. Lord Jesus, above all things, she longs for the day when her "feathers will shine like gold" in the glory reflected from your face. Amid the joyful glory of the saints, gleaming with your radiance, she will overflow with joy and be flooded with the light of your presence.

She has good reason to cry out, "His left hand is under my head, and his right hand embraces me!" His left hand is the thought of his incomparable love that moved him to lay down his life for his friends. His right hand is the blessed vision he has promised to his own, the great joy that they will have in his presence. The psalmist sings, "In your right hand, there are pleasures forever!" We are thus right in understanding the right hand to mean the divine and deifying joy of his presence. We are also right to see the left hand as representing the wonderful and unforgettable love that I have spoken of. We can never think about this love too much, for the bride lays her head upon the left hand and rests there until this sinful life passes away.

His left hand sustains the focus of her thoughts so that she is not drawn away from him by earthly desires, for the body wars against the spirit: "The corruptible body weighs heavily on the soul, and this earthy tent burdens the mind that muses on many things." However, she will rise from this burden if she rests upon the contemplation of mercy so astonishing and so undeserved, of love so free and so abundant, of kindness so enduring and unexpected, of forgiveness so complete, of grace so amazing.

The contemplation of these things will lift up the soul that meditates upon them. She will detach herself from all sinful attractions, reject everything that is inconsistent with God's great love, and yield herself entirely to heavenly things. Attracted by the sweetness of these rare perfumes, she will run eagerly to her lover. Although her heart is aflame with love, she considers her heart cold for offering so little in return for the great love of the bridegroom.

Indeed, when such a wonderful love comes down from on high, what does it matter that a speck of dust is consumed with gratitude and love for the great king who loved her first, who has revealed himself as fully devoted to the work of saving her? For "God so loved the world that he gave his one and only Son, that whoever believes in him shall not perish but have eternal life." This tells us about the love of God the Father. Of the Son, it is written, "he submitted himself to death." Of the Holy Spirit, Jesus says, "The helper, the Holy Spirit, whom the Father will send in my name, will teach you all things and bring to your remembrance all that I have said to you." In this, we see that God loves us and that he loves us with his entire being. If we may venture to speak of the infinite, incomprehensible being who is one and indivisible, the Holy Trinity loves us entirely and as one.

FIVE

Our Obligation to Love God

In considering what has been said so far, we see clearly that God should be loved and that he deserves our love. Unbelievers do not know the son of God, so they know neither the Father nor the Holy Spirit. "Whoever does not honor the Son does not honor the Father who sent him," nor do they honor the Holy Spirit whom he has sent. They know less of God than we do, so it is no surprise that they love God less. Even so, unbelievers still understand that they have and all that they are comes from their creator.

How then should it be for me? I cannot plead ignorance. I know that God made me without any merit of my own. I know that he provides all my needs, comforts me in my sorrow, and guides my footsteps with great care. Much more than that, I know that he is my redeemer, the author of eternal salvation, my treasure, and my glory. As it is written, "With him is abundant redemption," and again, "He entered the most holy place once for all by his own blood, thus obtaining eternal redemption."

Of his salvation, the psalmist says, "He will not forsake his saints. They are preserved forever." Of his abundant blessings, Luke says, "A good measure, pressed down, shaken together, and running over will be poured into your lap." Of the same, Paul says, "No eye has seen, no ear has heard, and no mind has imagined what God has prepared for those who love him." Of our glory, Paul also says, "But our citizenship is in heaven. And we eagerly await a Savior from there, the Lord Jesus Christ, who, by the power that enables him to bring everything under his control, will transform our lowly bodies so that they will be like his glorious body." And again:

"Our present sufferings are not worth comparing with the glory that will be revealed in us." And once more: "For our light and momentary troubles are achieving for us an eternal glory that far outweighs them all. So we fix our eyes not on what is seen but on what is unseen. What is seen is temporary, but what is unseen is eternal."

"How can I repay the Lord for all the good that he has done for me?" Reason and natural justice compel unbelievers to give themselves to the one who has given them their very being and to love him with all their strength. Because faith shows me that he has given me not only my own life but his life as well, I understand even more clearly that I must love him far more than I love myself.

Yet even before the day of Christian faith had dawned—before the Word became flesh, died on the cross, descended into hell, and rose to the Father—before God revealed how much he loved us through this great abundance of grace—even before the commandment had been uttered that "You shall love the Lord your God with all your heart and with all your soul and with all your might," that we must love him with all that we are, all that we know, and all that we can do—isn't God still justified in claiming this love from his own creations, the work of his hands? Shouldn't the work of art love its artist if it is able to do so? Shouldn't the creature love its creator with all its powers when it is only by the creator's grace that it has any power at all? Out of nothingness, God has called us into being and raised us up to the dignity of human beings. From this, we clearly see our obligation to love him entirely. We see his right to our love.

And how infinitely is the gift of God increased when we consider the fulfillment of the promise: "You, Lord, preserve both people and animals. How priceless is your unfailing love, O God!" For indeed, we "exchanged our glory for the image of an ox that eats grass." By our evil actions, we debased ourselves so that we became like irrational animals. If I owe all of myself to the one who *made* me, how can I ever pay my debt to the one who *remade* me — and in such an amazing way! It was a far less work to make than it was to remake. God had merely to speak the word and "at his command, they were created." But to repair the fall of the creation that came into being at his word — what words he had to speak, what miracles he had to perform, what cruelty and humiliation he had to suffer!

How can I repay the Lord for all the good that he has done for me? In his first creation, he gave me to myself. In his second creation, he gave himself to me and restored to me the self that I had lost. First made and then remade, given and then re-given, I owe myself to him twice over. But beyond that, what could I possibly offer God in return for the gift of himself? If I could give my whole being to him not twice but a thousand times over, what would that amount to compared to God?

Six

A Brief Summary

To briefly restate what's been said so far, we must first accept that God deserves to be greatly loved—infinitely loved—because he, the infinite, first loved us, miserable sinners that we are. He loved us freely and to excess, just as we are and without any claim whatsoever on our side, so as I said at the start, our love for him should have no limit. If the object of our love has no limits, how can we put limits on the love we owe him?

Moreover, our love is not a gift to him but the payment of a debt. He who loves us is the great *I Am*, eternal and immense, the divine love, the great God, whose greatness has no limits, whose wisdom knows know boundaries, whose peace "surpasses all human understanding." Because it is such a God as this who loves us, is it possible for us to say that we will love him up to a certain point and not beyond?

As the psalmist says, "I love you, Lord, my strength. The Lord is my rock, my fortress, and my deliverer. My God is my rock, in whom I take refuge." You are all that I need, all that my heart desires. My God and my help, I will love you for your goodness to me with all my strength — not as much as you deserve but as much as I am able.

I cannot love you as much as you deserve because I cannot love you more than my own feeble capacity allows. I will love you more when you grant me greater capacity for love, but I will never be able to love you as much as you should be loved. Your eyes see me as I am, for "your eyes saw my unformed body. All the days ordained for me were written in your book before one of them came to be." Yet in your book, you write the names of those who do what they can, even if they cannot do what they should.

I think I have said enough to show how much we should love God and that he deserves our love. But who really understands how much God deserves our love? Who has words for that?

Seven

The Benefits of Loving God

Let us now consider how we benefit from loving God. Our understanding of him falls far short of his great reality. Even so, we must not keep silent about what we do see just because we do not see everything. Earlier, when I spoke about why and to what degree we should love God, I said that there were two possible meanings to the question at hand—why God deserves our love and how we benefit from his love. It seems that you are asking both questions, so having spoken first of why God deserves our love, not as well as he deserves but as well as we are able, it remains that as well as his grace allows, I should now speak about the rewards of his love.

Even though God should be loved without any thought of a reward, God nonetheless does reward us for our love. True love cannot be left destitute, but neither can it be considered mercenary, for it "does not insist on its own way." Love is an affection, not a contract. It cannot be given or received through negotiated agreements. It moves within us freely, making us spontaneous. Love is its own satisfaction, and that reward lies in its beloved. Whatever we may seem to love, if we love it on account of something else, it is really the something else that we love and not the thing that we seem to love. Paul, for example, did not preach the gospel in order to have something to eat. He ate so that he would have the strength to preach the gospel. He loved the gospel, not the bread. True love seeks no reward, but it deserves one.

A reward is offered to the one who does not yet love. It is owed to the one who loves. It is given to the one who perseveres in love. In lesser matters, it is not the willing but the unwilling whom we woo with promises of rewards. Who would think of paying people to do something they already yearn to do? No one pays a starving person to eat, or a thirsty person to drink, or a mother to nurse her hungry child. Who would think of bribing people to fence their own vineyards, till their own orchards, or build their own houses? Much more, then, do those who truly love God require no other reward than God himself. If they were to seek any further reward, it would be the reward that they loved, not God.

It is natural for people to desire things they do not have when those things appear to be better than the things that they do have. It is natural for them to be dissatisfied when the things they have lack the particular qualities that they prefer. Thus, if a man prefers his wife because of her beauty, his eyes will long for a woman who is more beautiful. If he clothes himself with expensive clothing, he will covet clothing that is more expensive. No matter how rich he is, he will envy those who are richer than he.

Don't we see this every day? People of great wealth and immense property add field upon field, dreaming of even greater estates. Those who live in houses worthy of kings are forever adding house upon house, continually building up and tearing down, making squares into circles and circles into squares. And what about people promoted to high positions? Don't we see them continually striving to rise higher and higher out of insatiable ambition? There is no end to such restless desire because no one thing can be defined as absolutely the highest or the best. It is no wonder, then, that as a long as people can see something higher and better sitting just outside their reach, they will never be satisfied with the lower and worse things they already possess.

What madness to forever long for things that can neither satisfy nor even reduce their desires. No matter how many things they have, they are dissatisfied. They long for what is missing. They lust for the things they do not have. Thus these restless minds scurry about amongst the unreal pleasures of this world, wearying themselves with pointless labors, always craving more, never appreciating all that they have. They are like the starving man who thinks that whatever he puts in his mouth is nothing compared to all that remains to be eaten. He anxiously wants what he does not yet have rather than enjoying what he has.

But who can hope to own all things? Even the little that one person can own is only obtained with great labor and enjoyed with trembling, for we know with certainty that all will be lost on the day that God has appointed but kept hidden from view. Thus the perverse will struggles to obtain the finest things, rushing forward toward whatever will give it the greatest satisfaction — but all for nothing. Vanity toys with the will with its crooked paths. The sinful will deceives itself with lies. If you really want to have what you desire, to take hold of the one thing that leaves nothing to be desired, then why bother with all these lesser things? When you do that, you run on crooked paths, and you will die long before you reach the thing that you truly desire.

Thus the worldly wander about in circles, longing for something to satisfy their desires but foolishly rejecting the only thing that can bring them true satisfaction, which is not a matter of consumption but of consummation. Their lives are consumed by useless labors, never achieving the perfect happiness they seek, because they seek the beauty of created things, not the creator. They search for happiness by trying everything, one thing after another, never dreaming of going to the Lord who made them all.

If they were somehow able to achieve their heart's desire and take possession of the entire world — but without possessing the one who is its author — then by the same law that has ruled their lives, they would ultimately condemn all that they possess and restlessly long for the one thing they lack, God himself. Only there will they find rest. Just as there is no rest on this side of eternity, so on the other side, nothing can disturb their rest. Then they can say with confidence, "But as for me, it is good to be near God." They will even add, "Whom have I in heaven but you? And there is nothing on earth that I desire besides you." And also: "God is the strength of my heart and my portion forever." Thus, as I have said, those who desire the greatest good could reach it if they could first obtain all the things in this world that fall short of that greatest good.

However, that is impossible. Life is too short. Our strength is too feeble. Our temptations are too many. Those who struggle forward are exhausted by the length of these crooked paths and the futility of their struggle. They want to have everything they desire, but they cannot reach the end of their desires. It would be far better for them to test all things in thought rather than experiencing them first-hand. They could easily do this, and it would not be for nothing, for the mind is swift and sharper than the senses. It races before them, while they do not dare to even touch a thing unless the mind has first examined and approved it.

I believe that this is what is meant by "test all things and hold on to what is good." The mind looks ahead, and unless it gives its approval, the senses cannot pursue what they desire. Otherwise, you may not "ascend the mountain of the Lord" or "stand in his holy place." You will gain nothing from having received the gift of reason. You would follow the impulses of your senses like an animal, and your dormant reason would offer no resistance. Those who do not think may indeed run a race, but they don't run on the right path. The spurn the apostle's advice that they should "run to win the prize." They will never reach the finish line — the Lord — because they don't want to reach him until they have first tried everything else. Their desire to first possess everything is like a circle. It goes on forever.

The righteous are not like this. Hearing about the multitude who run around in circles — "for the gate is wide and the way is easy that leads to destruction, and those who enter by it are many" — they choose the royal highway and stray neither to the right nor the left. The prophet also testifies: "The path of the righteous is level. You, the Upright One, make the way of the righteous smooth." The righteous travel directly to their destination. They avoid the dangerous, unsatisfying, round-about paths by choosing the brief and abbreviating Word. They do not desire to have everything they see but sell everything they own and give it to the poor, for truly, "blessed are the poor because theirs is the kingdom of heaven."

Everyone runs in a race, but we must distinguish between the types of runners, "for the Lord watches over the path of the righteous, but the path of the wicked will perish." Therefore, "Better is the little that the righteous has than the abundance of many wicked." As wisdom says and the fool discovers, "The one who loves money is never satisfied with money, and whoever loves wealth is never satisfied with wealth." But as Christ says, "Blessed are those who hunger and thirst for righteousness, for they will be satisfied."

Righteousness is the natural and essential food of the soul. The hunger of the soul can no more be satisfied by earthly treasures than the hunger of the body can be satisfied by air. If you were to see a starving man open his mouth and puff up his cheeks with gusts of wind to satisfy his hunger, you would think him a fool. It is no less foolish to imagine that the soul will be satisfied and not merely puffed up with the things of this world.

What do material things mean to the soul? What do ideas mean to the body? The body cannot be satisfied by spiritual things, and the soul cannot be satisfied by the things of this world. As the psalmist says, "Praise the Lord, O my soul! He satisfies your desires with good things." He satisfies your soul with good things. He urges it toward goodness. He guards it in goodness. He anticipates, sustains, and fulfills.

He fills your soul with desire, and he is the fulfillment of your soul's desire.

I have said already that the reason to love God is God himself. I spoke truly, for he is both the source of love and the ultimate object of love. He himself provides the opportunity for love. He himself creates the desire to love and fulfills that desire. He makes — or rather, has made — himself such that he should be loved. He hopes to be so happily loved that no one will ever love him in vain. His love prepares our love and rewards it. He leads the way with gentleness, rewarding us justly. He is our hope, "richly blessing all who call on him," although he can give us nothing better than himself. He gave himself to earn us. He keeps himself as our reward. He provides himself as food for righteous souls. He sold himself to ransom those in captivity.

O Lord, you are so good to the soul that seeks you! What then will you be to the soul who finds you? And this is the more amazing thing, that no one can seek you who has not already found you. You wish to be found so that you can be sought, and you wish to be sought so that you can be found. But while you can be sought and found, you cannot be put off. Even if we say, "in the morning my prayer comes before you," we must remember that our prayers become half-hearted unless you first inspire them.

Now that we have looked at where our love finishes, let us look at where it begins.

EIGHT

The First Stage of Love

Love is one of the four natural passions, which do not need to be named here because they are well known. It is fitting, then, that what is natural in humans should be the first to serve the author of nature. That is why the first and greatest commandment is to "Love the Lord your God with all your heart and with all your soul and with all your mind."

Human nature has become so fragile and weak that people are driven to love themselves first. This is worldly love, by which people love themselves first and for their own sake. They think only of themselves. As Paul writes, "The spiritual did not come first, but the natural, and after that the spiritual." This love does not come through any discipline. It is a natural part of humans, for "no people ever hated their own body." However, if this same love grows excessive—as it often does—and, refusing to stay within the restraining banks of it needs, overflows into the fields of pleasure, then a command can stop the flood: "'Love your neighbor as yourself."

This is as it should be, for those who share our human nature should not be deprived of its benefits, and particularly of the love that is essential to human nature. If people find it difficult to help others in both their needs and their pleasures, they must restrain their own desires or else they will fall into sin. They can indulge themselves as much as they like, but only if they remember to offer the same tolerance to their neighbors. The law of life and order requires this restraint to keep you from chasing after your own desires until you perish. It prevents your lusts from transforming this natural goodness into slavery to the enemy of your soul. Wouldn't it be better to share the goodness of human nature with your neighbor than with your enemy?

Follow the counsel of wisdom to "control your desires lest they control you." Follow the example of the apostle as well: "If we have food and shelter, we will be satisfied with that." If you do so, you will soon find it easy to protect your love from "the worldly desires that wage war against your soul." You will not find it burdensome to share with your neighbors what you have held back from the enemy of your soul. When you refuse to indulge your desires in order to give your neighbors what they need, your natural love will be reasonable and just. Thus our natural, selfish love becomes social when we offer it to the community.

What are you to do if, by sharing what you have with your neighbor, you yourself are left lacking what is necessary? What else can you do but pray with confidence to God, "who gives to all generously and without reproach" and who opens his hand to "satisfy the desires of every living thing"? Because he gives so generously in times of abundance, there is no doubt he will also give generously in times of need. Scripture tells us to "seek the kingdom of God above all else, and he will give you everything you need." Without being asked, God promises to provide all the necessities to those who love their neighbors, who do not hold back for themselves the things that their neighbors need. This is what it means to seek the kingdom of God and ask for his help to overcome the tyranny of sin, to accept the yoke of chastity and sobriety instead of allowing sin to "reign in your mortal body." And again, it is only right that you should share the gifts of human nature with those who share that nature with you.

However, if we are to love our neighbors with perfect justice, we must first abide in God. How can you love your neighbors purely if you do not love them in God? And you cannot love in God unless you first love God himself. Then, as you abide in God, you can love your neighbors as well. God thus creates your love for him just as he creates all other good things.

He does so as follows. He who made the natural world also protects it. It was created in such a way that it requires its creator to be its protector as well. The world would not exist without its creator, and it could not continue to exist apart from him. In order that reasonable creatures like ourselves should not be ignorant of this or vainly attribute to themselves the gifts from their creator, God has chosen — in his high and saving wisdom — that humans should be disciplined by tribulations. Thus, when people fail and God comes to their rescue, they will give to God the honor he deserves. Of this, he says, "Call upon me in the day of trouble. I will rescue you, and you will honor me." In this way, people, who are physical animals and only able to love themselves, begin to love God for their own benefit. They learn that when they abide in God, they can do all things that are good for themselves and that apart from him, they can do nothing.

NINE

The Second and
Third Stages of Love

People love God, therefore, but they love him because of the help he offers and not because of who he is. Even so, it is wise to understand what you can do on your own and what you can do only with God's help. You will then avoid offending the one who keeps you safe from sin. However, if the trials of this life become more frequent, thus driving you to call on God more often, then even if you had a breast of iron or a heart of stone, wouldn't you be softened by the goodness of such a savior and love him not just for what he offers you but for his own sake?

Our frequent trials and needs compel us to call upon God more often, and this closer contact allows us to "taste and see that the Lord is good." Tasting this sweetness of the Lord draws us away from loving him selfishly because of the help he offers and brings us into a more pure love. The Samaritans illustrate this when they tell the woman, "We no longer believe just because of what you said. Now we have heard for ourselves, and we know that this man really is the savior of the world." We offer the same testimony when we follow their example and say to our own lives in this world, "We no longer love God because of how he meets all of our needs but because we have tasted and seen how good the Lord is."

Our lives in this world have a way of talking—through our actions—about the goodness we have tasted. It becomes easy to obey the commandment to love our neighbors because whoever loves God truthfully will love everything that belongs to God. We love purely, and to the pure, it is no burden to obey the commandments. As it is written, "in obedience to the truth, we have purified our souls for a sincere love." We love justly, and thus we are eager to obey God's just commandment.

This love is sweet because it is freely given. It is pure because it is not love "in word or talk but in deed and in truth." It is just because it gives back what it has been given. All who love in this way offer love because they are loved. They no longer love for their own benefit but for the sake of Jesus, just as Jesus did not give himself for his own benefit but for ours—or rather, for our very selves. All who love in this way join the psalmist in singing, "Give thanks to the Lord, for he is good!" They praise God not because God is good to them but because God is good. They love God not for their own sake but for his. When the psalmist wrote "he will praise you when you do him favors," he was not speaking of this kind of love.

This then is the third stage of love, loving God for his own sake.

TEN

The Fourth Stage of Love

How happy are those who reach the fourth stage of love! At this stage, they only love themselves for God's sake.

"O God, your righteousness is like the mountains of God!" This kind of love is a mountain, a high mountain of God, a rich and fertile mountain: "Who may ascend the mountain of the Lord?" Also: "Oh, that I had the wings of a dove! I would fly away and be at rest." This place was created as a place of peace, "his dwelling place in Zion."

Alas for me, my exile continues. When will this flesh and blood, this clay dish, this earthly house, experience such love? When will I know this kind of love so that the mind, drunk with divine love, will forget itself, see itself as a broken dish, and throw itself entirely upon God, clinging to him, becoming one with him in spirit, saying, "My flesh and my heart have wasted away. You are the God of my heart, the God who is my portion forever."

I consider anyone who experiences love of this sort — so rare in this life — to be blessed and holy, even if this experience only lasts for a moment. To lose yourself as though you no longer existed, to be emptied entirely of yourself, to have no sense of yourself at all, is not a human emotion but divine love.

However, if any mortals are seized by this heavenly joy and admitted, even for a moment, into this union with God, the world immediately calls them back. The troubles of the day disturb them. Their bodies weigh them down. The desires of the flesh bother them. They fail because of the weakness of their corruption. And more powerfully than any of that, brotherly love calls them back to duty. Alas, they must return to their lives in this world, to descend back into themselves, and wretchedly cry out, "O Lord, I am oppressed! Help me!" and, "Wretched person that I am! Who will rescue me from this body of death?"

Because the scripture says that God "has made everything for his own purposes," the day will come when God will make everything conform to his will and exist in harmony with him. Until that day comes, we must make this our goal, too. Just as God has chosen everything for his own purposes, so we must desire that nothing—not even ourselves—should exist for our own pleasure but only for him.

True happiness will not be found in the satisfaction of our desires or momentary pleasures but in seeing God's will fulfilled in us and through us. We ask for this every day when we pray: "Your will be done, on earth as it is in heaven." O pure and holy love! O sweet and tender affection! O pure and sinless intention of the will, all the more pure and sinless because it has been thoroughly washed and purged of any selfishness, all the more sweet and tender because everything within it is divine.

To experience this kind of love is to become like God. As a drop of water seems to disappear entirely in a vessel of wine, taking upon itself the color and flavor of the wine, or as red, molten iron becomes so much like the fire around it that it seems to have lost its first state, or as the air of a sunny day seems to be so filled with sunlight that it is not merely lit up but light itself—so in all saints, it happens that human feelings mysteriously melt away and flow into the will of God. How could God "be all in all" if anything merely human remained in humans? The substance remains, but it takes another form, a greater glory, another power.

When will that be? Who will see this? Who will possess it? "When shall I come and appear before God?" O my Lord, my God, "You have said, 'Seek my face.' My heart says to you, 'Your

61

face, Lord, do I seek.'" O Lord, do you think that I, even I, will see your holy temple?

I do not think that we can fully and perfectly obey that commandment—"Love the Lord your God with all your heart and with all your soul and with all your mind and with all your strength." In this life, the mind and heart must consider the body. The soul must give life and feeling to flesh. But when the soul is finally freed from these constraints, its strength will be established in the power of God. It is thus impossible for us to gather up all that is within us and seek the face of God as long as we must also give our attention to the care of these weak and miserable bodies of ours.

The soul can only hope to possess the fourth stage of love—or rather, to be possessed by it, for it is in God's hands to give this to those he chooses—when it has been clothed with a spiritual and immortal body, a perfect body, calm and pleasant and in all ways obedient to the spirit. No human effort can attain this degree of love, but we will easily reach that highest stage of love when we are no longer held back by the desires of our earthly bodies or disturbed by the troubles of this world.

However, may we not suppose that the holy martyrs enjoyed this grace, at least in part, before they laid down their victorious bodies? The great force of this love took hold of their souls so entirely that they were able to expose their bodies to outward torments and think nothing of them. The physical pain may have disturbed their peace of mind, but it could not overcome them.

ELEVEN

After the Resurrection

What about the souls who have already been released from their bodies? We believe that they are fully immersed in a vast sea of eternal light and of everlasting brightness. However, no one denies that they want to have their bodies again. If they thus still hope and desire to receive their bodies, then clearly they have not completely turned away from themselves. They still cling to something that is their own, however slight. Until "death has been swallowed up in victory" and eternal light invades and overwhelms the farthest boundaries of night, filling all things so that eternal glory shines even in those bodies, souls cannot be completely freed from self and able to give themselves up entirely to God. They remain attached to their bodies, if not by life and feeling then by a natural affection, and thus they do not want—nor are they able—to attain to their perfect consummation without them.

Thus the consummation of the soul, which is its highest state, cannot take place before the resurrection of the body. If the soul could attain this consummation without the body, it would no longer desire to be united with the body, and the body is neither set aside nor resumed unless it benefits the soul. As it is written, "Precious in the sight of the Lord is the death of his saints." If death is precious, then what must life be—and such a life as theirs?

It should not surprise us that the resurrected body should seem to offer something to the soul, for the body was of great help when the person was weak and mortal. How truly the apostle spoke when he said that "in all things God works for the good of those who love him." The body is of great help to the soul that loves God, even when it is ill, even when it is dead, and all the more when it is raised again from the dead. In illness, the body teaches the soul patience. In death, it gives the soul peace. In resurrection, it brings the soul perfect consummation. Naturally, then, the soul does not want to be perfected without the body, for it recognizes the good service of the body in every condition.

The body is clearly a good and faithful companion for a good soul. It helps when the soul is burdened. It relieves the soul when it cannot help. It is a benefit, certainly, and not itself a burden. The first condition is full of labor but fruitful labor. The second condition is a time of waiting but of waiting without weariness. The third condition is entirely glorious. Listen to the bridegroom in the Song of Songs offering us this three-part invitation: "Eat, friends, drink, and be drunk, my beloved!" Those who are still laboring in their bodies, he invites to eat. Those who have set aside their bodies in death, he invites to drink. Those who have resumed their resurrected bodies, he invites to be drunk, calling them his "beloved" because they are filled to overflowing with love.

There is a difference between those he calls "beloved" and those he calls "friends." Those who still labor away in their bodies are dear to him because of the love they have for him. Those who have been released from the burden of the flesh are more dear because they are now more ready and able to love him. However, the last ones are the dearest, for they are clothed in the glory of resurrected bodies. Nothing remains to trouble them or hold them back in any way. They can give themselves eagerly and entirely to the love of God. Neither of the first two conditions can claim that, for in first, the soul must carry the weight of the body, and in the second, it waits for the body as something missing.

In the first condition, then, the faithful soul eats its bread, but it does so, alas, "by the sweat of its brow." Living in the body, it must walk by faith, and faith must work in love, for "faith without works is dead." This work is food for the soul, just as the Lord says: "My food is to do the will of the one who sent me."

When the body is laid aside, the soul no longer eats the bread of sorrow. Having eaten, it is allowed to drink deeply from the wine of love. However, the wine is not yet pure wine, for as the bride says in the Song of Solomon, "I drank my wine with my milk." The soul mixes the wine of divine love with the milk of natural emotion that still desires to have the body back in its glorified state. The soul glows with the warmth of the wine of love but not to the point of drunkenness. The milk tempers the power of wine for the time being. Intoxication overpowers the mind and makes it forget everything, even itself, but the soul that still waits for the resurrection of its body has not forgotten itself entirely.

Once that final desire is fulfilled, what could hinder the soul from yielding itself entirely to God, ceasing to be like itself even more as it is more and more like God? Only then is the soul allowed to drink from the cup of wisdom's pure wine, as it is written: "How good is my cup that intoxicates me!" Is it any wonder if the soul is then intoxicated by the riches of God's home? Free from all worldly cares, it can drink pure, new wine with Christ in his father's house.

Wisdom presides over this three-course banquet of love, feeding those who labor, giving refreshment to those who rest, and intoxicating those who reign with Christ. Just as with meals in this world, the food is served first and then the wine. This is the order that nature requires, and wisdom follows it. As long as we are alive in this world, laboring in our bodies, we eat the work of our hands, laboriously chewing what has to be swallowed. After death, when we enter our spiritual life, we drink whatever we are offered in comfort. Finally, after our bodies are resurrected, we are intoxicated by eternal life, overflowing with wonderful abundance. This is what the bridegroom means when he says, "Eat, friends, drink, and be drunk, my beloved!" Eat before death, drink after death, and drink abundantly after the resurrection.

It is right to call them "beloved" when they are drunk with love, and it is right for them to drink abundantly when they deserve to be brought to the marriage feast of the Lord, eating and drinking at his table and in his kingdom as he presents his bride "to himself as a radiant church, without stain or wrinkle or any other blemish." In every way, he will then intoxicate his beloved ones with "the river of his delights." In that most passionate and holy embrace of the bridegroom and bride, the force of the river will "make the city of God rejoice." I think this refers to what was promised by the son of God, who comes to us and serves us: "The righteous will be glad. They will rejoice before God. They will be filled with joy!"

Here is fullness without disgust. Here is endless curiosity without discontent. Here is endless and eternal desire that has all it seeks. Here is sober intoxication of truth that does not come from overdrinking, that does not stink of wine, but that comes from a burning desire for God. From this point forward, the fourth stage of love lasts forever. We love God alone in the highest way because we no longer love ourselves except for his sake. He himself is the reward for those who love him, the eternal reward for an eternal love.

Twelve

Perfect Love

I remember writing a letter to the holy Carthusians some time back. In it, I discussed these same stages of love—along with other matters. I may have shared some other thoughts about love in it, just as I have talked about love here. For that reason, I think it might be useful to include the letter here. It is also easier to copy what I have already written than to compose something new.

True and sincere love proceeds from "a pure heart, a good conscience, and a sincere faith." It makes us care as much about our neighbor's welfare as our own. Those who love themselves mostly—or entirely—do not purely love goodness. They love goodness because it benefits them, not for its own sake. They cannot obey the prophet when he says, "Give thanks to the Lord, for he is good!" They may give thanks to the Lord because he is good to them but not because he is himself good. The same prophet has this reproach for them: "As long as God does good to them, they will acknowledge him."

Some praise God because he is powerful. Some praise God because God is good to them. Some praise God simply because he is good. The first are slaves who fear for themselves. The second are hirelings who think only of themselves. The third are children who honor their father. Those who fear and those who are greedy praise God for their own benefit. Only those who love like children "do not insist on their own way." The following passage refers to this kind of love: "The law of the Lord is perfect, restoring the soul," for it alone can turn the mind away from loving the world or loving itself and focus it on loving God.

Neither fear nor self-love can restore the soul. From time to time, they may change one's outward appearance or one's actions, but they can never change one's character. Slaves may sometimes do the work of God, but because they don't do it from their own free will, they remain slaves. Hirelings may sometimes do the work of God as well, but because they do so for their own reward, they continue to be driven by their greed. Wherever there is self-interest, there is a desire for special treatment. That desire is like the dark corner of a room, and in those corners you find rust and dirt. Let the slaves, then, have their own law, which is the very fear that enslaves them. Let the hirelings have their greed, which holds them back when temptation entices and pulls at them. But neither of these is perfect, so neither will restore souls. Only love restores souls because only love makes them willing.

I call this love perfect because it holds back nothing of its own for itself. If people hold back nothing as their own, then everything they own

belongs to God—and everything that belongs
to God is holy and good. The perfect law of God
is the kind of love that does not seek its own
welfare but the welfare of others. It is called the
law of God because God himself lives according
to it and because no human can possess it except
as a gift from him. I don't find it absurd to say
that God himself lives according to a law because
that law is simply love. What else preserves the
glorious and unutterable unity of the holy and
blessed Trinity except love? Love then is the law,
the law of the Lord, which somehow unites and
holds the Trinity in "the bond of peace."

Don't think that I imply that love exists as
merely a quality or a kind of accident in God.
If I were to say that—and far be it from me
to do so—it would imply that there is something within God that is not God. No, love is
the very substance of God, and this is not a new
or extraordinary thought, for as John says, "God
is love." We can honestly say then that love is at
once God and the gift of God. Thus love gives

love. The substance of love imparts the quality of love. When this word refers to the giver, it refers to the substance, the very nature of God. When the word refers to the gift, it means the character that God imparts.

Love is the eternal law that creates and governs the universe. All things were made in size, weight, and number according to this law. Nothing exists outside of it. Even the law does not exist apart from law, apart from itself. Love does not create itself, but it governs itself by its own law.

THIRTEEN

The Slave and the Hireling

The slave and the hireling have a law of their own that does not come from God. The slave does not love God. The hireling loves something else more than God.

They have a law of their own, but even that law remains subject to the law of the Lord. We can all make laws for ourselves, but we cannot supplant the unchanging order of the eternal law. We create our own law when we put our own will ahead of the general, eternal law. In a perverse way, we imitate our creator. Just as God is a law unto himself, depending entirely upon himself, we too want to be entirely independent and make our own will the only law we follow.

Alas, this unbearable yoke weighs heavily on all the children of Adam, bowing our necks and twisting our spines, bringing our lives down to hell: "Wretched man that I am! Who will deliver me from this body of death?" It weighs me down, almost crushing me, so that "If the Lord had not been my help, my soul would soon have lived in the land of silence."

Weighed down by this burden, Job groans, "Why have you made me your target so that I have become a burden to myself?" When he says "so that I have become a burden to myself," he shows that he has been a law unto himself and that this is his own doing. But first, speaking to God, he says, "Why have you made me your target?" This shows that he could not escape God's law.

It is the nature of the eternal and just law of God that whoever refuses to be ruled gently by love will suffer under the bitter tyranny of self. Those who refuse the easy yoke and light burden of love must struggle—against their will—under the heavy yoke of their own self-will. In this mysterious and just way, the eternal law of love captures those who flee from it or oppose it and at the same time keeps them under its rule. They remain subject to the just power of the law, but they are exiled from its happiness because they cannot dwell in the light, the rest, and the glory of God.

O Lord, my God, "Why don't you pardon my offenses and forgive my sins?" If you would do that, then I would be freed from the heavy burden of my own will. I could breathe freely under the light burden of love, not coerced by slavish fear or drawn on by the greed of the hireling but led by the your Holy Spirit, the Spirit of freedom. He guides your children and assures me that I too am one of your children, that the same law of love applies to us both, and that in this world, I will be like you. The apostle says, "Owe no one anything, except to love each other." Those who follow this guidance are truly like God. They are neither slaves nor hirelings but children.

FOURTEEN

The Law of Love

The children do not live outside the law — unless perhaps someone wants to give a different interpretation to this text: "The law is not made for those who are good." However, you must understand that the law of fear that comes with slavery is different from the law of gentleness that comes with freedom. Children are not required to obey the law of fear, but they could not survive without the law of freedom.

Do you want to know why there is no law for those who are good? Paul writes, "You did not receive the spirit of slavery to fall back into fear." Do you want to know why the children are not outside the law of love? "But you have received the Spirit of adoption as children." Listen to Paul explain how he is neither under the law nor free from the law: "To those under the law, I became like one under the law — though not being myself under the law — so I might win those who are under the law. To those outside the law, I became like one outside the law — though not being outside the law of God but under the law of Christ — so I might win those outside the law."

It is thus incorrect to say that those who are good have no law or that they are outside the law but that "the law is not made for those who are good." In other words, the law is not imposed on them unwillingly. Inspired by goodness, they willingly accept what is given to them. Thus the Lord says fittingly, "Take my yoke upon you." It's as if he were to say, "I don't force this yoke upon the unwilling. If you desire it, then take it. Otherwise, you'll only find weariness instead of rest for your souls."

The law of love is good and pleasant. It's not only easy to bear, but it even makes the laws of the slave and the hireling bearable because it does not destroy them but fulfills them. As Jesus says, "I have not come to take the law away but to fulfill it." It tempers the fear of the slave, and it regulates the desires of the hireling, lightening the burdens of both. Love does not remove fear, but it becomes a godly fear. Love does not remove worldly desires, but they become lawful desires.

Thus love fulfills the law of the slave by bringing devotion to the slave. It fulfills the law of the hireling by restraining greed. Devotion mixed with fear does not destroy fear, but it purifies the fear. It removes the punishment. The law of the slave could not function without the fear of punishment. When the punishment is removed, the fear remains, but it becomes a pure, child's fear. When we read, "perfect love drives out fear," we must understand this to mean the punishment that is always a part of the fear of the slave. It is a figure of speech that gives the effect in place of the cause.

The arrival of love also restrains greed. Love causes the hireling to reject evil entirely and to prefer the better things to those that are merely good. It desires the good only for the sake of the better. When, by the grace of God, this is fully realized, they will only love their bodies and all its good things for the sake of their souls, their souls for the sake of God, and God for his own sake.

FIFTEEN

The Four Stages of Love

Because we are human and born out of the
desires of the flesh, it is unavoidable that our
desires and love should begin with our bodies.
However, when it is properly guided, love will
proceed by the grace of God through these stages
until it is consummated in the spirit.

As it is written, "The spiritual did not come
first, but the physical, and after that the spiritual." It was necessary for us to first bear "the
image of an earthy being" before we could bear
"the image of a heavenly being." At first, then,
we love ourselves for our own sake because we
are physical creatures and cannot see anything
beyond our own existence.

However, we gradually perceive that we cannot be the authors of ourselves, so by faith we begin to seek after God and even to love him as something necessary for our own welfare. In this second stage of love, we love God for our sake and not for his. However, after our own needs lead us to honor God and come before him by thinking of him, reading about him, praying to him, and obeying him, God begins to reveal himself to us. As our familiarity increases, our love increases. We taste the sweetness of God.

Having "tasted and seen that the Lord is good," we advance to the third stage of love. We love God not as our benefactor but as God. We undoubtedly remain at this third stage for a long time. I doubt that we ever really attain the fourth stage—loving God for his sake only—in this lifetime.

If others have experienced the fourth stage, they can speak to it. To me, it seems impossible. However, I am confident that it will indeed take place when the good and faithful servant "enters into the joy of the master" and is intoxicated by "the abundance of God's house." In some miraculous way, we will forget ourselves entirely. We will no longer belong to our former lives. Leaving ourselves behind, we will unite with God, becoming "one with him in spirit."

I believe this is what the prophet saw when he said, "I will enter into the power of the Lord. O Lord, I will be mindful of your justice alone." The prophet understood that when he enters into the spiritual power of God, he will leave behind all the weakness and distraction of the body, no longer giving a thought to the world. Living entirely in his spirit, he will see nothing but the righteousness of God.

On that day, every Christian can say what Paul says about Christ: "Though we once regarded Christ from a human point of view, we do so no longer." No one in heaven knows Christ from a human point of view because "flesh and blood cannot inherit the kingdom of God." This does not mean that the resurrected substance of the body will not be present in heaven. This means that all worldly needs will disappear. Human love will be absorbed by spiritual love. The weak, human feelings we carry now will become divine.

The net of love "that was thrown into the great wide sea and gathered fish of every kind" will be pulled to shore. The good will be kept, and the bad will be thrown aside. In this new life, God's all-encompassing love gathers every kind of fish in the wide folds of its net. It wraps itself around us, drawing into itself the adversity and prosperity of everyone. This love makes us all its own, "rejoicing with those who rejoice, weeping with those who weep." However, when the net is finally pulled to shore, everything that we have suffered will be thrown away like rotten fish. God will only keep what pleases him and offers you joy.

On that day, will Paul continue to feel weak with those who are weak or burn with anger at scandal when neither weakness nor scandal exist? Will he grieve over sinners who refuse to repent when there is neither the sinner nor the repentant? When Paul is in that city whose rushing river brings joy and whose gates the Lord loves "more than all the other dwellings of Jacob," there can no weeping for those condemned to "the eternal fire prepared for the devil and his angels."

Even though there are some victories in this life and we can rejoice, we always have more battles to fight, more danger to face. But in that final home of ours, there will be no more sorrow or adversity. As it is written, "The home of all who rejoice is in you." And again, "They shall have everlasting joy." How could we turn our thoughts toward mercy when we are "mindful of God's justice alone"? When there is no place for misery and no time for mercy, there will be no feelings of compassion.

www.ingramcontent.com/pod-product-compliance
Lightning Source LLC
Chambersburg PA
CBHW021937040426